The Immortal Fortune

The Immortal Fortune

Matthew Petchinsky

1

The Immortal Fortune: Secret Wealth Lessons from Captain Jack Harkness

By: Matthew Petchinsky

Disclaimer

This book, ***The Immortal Fortune: Secret Wealth Lessons from Captain Jack Harkness***, is a **fan-made creation** inspired by the fictional character Captain Jack Harkness as depicted in the television series *Doctor Who* and its spin-off *Torchwood*. Captain Jack Harkness is the intellectual property of the BBC and related rights holders. This work is **not licensed, authorized, endorsed, or affiliated** with the BBC, the creators of *Doctor Who*, or any official franchise entities.

The concepts, themes, and lessons presented throughout this book are **metaphorical, symbolic, and educational in nature**. References to Captain Jack Harkness, his adventures, or his fictional immortality are used strictly as creative analogies to explore ideas about resilience, long-term thinking, hidden strength, and adaptive wealth-building. They are not meant to suggest any canonical truths about the character, nor to substitute for the rich storytelling of the official *Doctor Who* and *Torchwood* series.

All strategies, scenarios, and examples contained in this book are provided for **inspiration and entertainment purposes only**. They do not constitute financial, legal, tax, or investment advice. Readers are encouraged to treat the material as a framework for **imaginative exploration** rather than a guide to actual monetary decisions. Any application of these ideas in real-world contexts should be undertaken only after consulting qualified professionals in the relevant fields.

By reading this work, you acknowledge and accept that the author and publisher make **no guarantees of financial outcomes or personal success**, and disclaim all liability for actions taken based on the contents herein.

This book is, above all else, a **celebration of creativity, fandom, and metaphorical thinking** — a way to reimagine the lessons of a beloved character in the realm of personal growth and imaginative wealth-building.

Introduction — The Time Traveler's Bank Account

Captain Jack Harkness isn't just immortal in body — he is immortal in mindset. From the coal-smoked streets of 1869, where fortunes were forged in steam and steel, to the neon-lit economies of today, where fortunes rise and collapse in a digital heartbeat, Jack has lived through every upheaval, crash, and revolution. Yet through it all, one truth has guided his survival: **true wealth is not in what you flash, but in what you quietly protect, compound, and carry forward into the next era.**

Most people think of wealth in short cycles — a paycheck, a quarter, a single booming year. Jack thinks in centuries. He knows how to turn a single coin into a silent empire by playing the long game, hiding wealth where no one thinks to look, and letting time itself become his most faithful business partner. His life teaches us that survival isn't about luck — it's about structure, secrecy, and patience.

This book does not pretend you can live forever, but it does reveal how to **adapt "immortal wealth strategies" into modern life.** You don't need two centuries of lifespan to learn from Jack. You only need his perspective: that every dollar saved and shielded today is a soldier in an army that grows stronger tomorrow. That living well doesn't mean flaunting — it means disguising. That prosperity endures best when built quietly, invisibly, and steadily, across decades.

Through Jack's lens, we'll explore the art of invisible affluence: how to enjoy glamour without exposure, how to spot hidden opportunities that others overlook, and how to shield your prosperity from envy, taxes, and turbulence. We'll study resilience in times of war, recession, and collapse, and learn how to always have a reserve — a hidden bank account of time-tested wealth — when others falter.

What you will gain in these pages is not a manual for flashy riches but a blueprint for **becoming secretly rich, forever.** You'll learn to think like an immortal time traveler who knows that every setback can be turned into a compounding advantage, that the real currency of power is patience, and that the truest luxury is to walk through the world with wealth no one can see — but that always works for you in silence.

Welcome to *The Immortal Fortune*. Your journey into the Time Traveler's Bank Account begins here.

Chapter 1: The Centuries Game — Wealth That Outlives You

Captain Jack Harkness has walked through more economic eras than most history books cover. He has seen fortunes made in coal, squandered in the stock market crash of 1929, multiplied during the digital revolution, and reinvented with every war, peace treaty, and global boom. The lesson he carries is simple but profound: **true wealth is not measured by the noise it makes today but by the silence it keeps while compounding across decades.**

Most people chase quick wins. They want the lucky gamble, the viral moment, the instant fortune. Jack knows better. For him, a hundred years is just another playing field. If a single gold coin tucked away in 1869 can grow into a mountain by 1969, and into an empire by 2069, then the game isn't about speed — it's about **endurance, patience, and time itself working as an ally.**

The Power of Compounding Time

The average person thinks in days and months. The wealthy think in years. Jack thinks in centuries. Compounding is the closest thing mortals have to time travel: the longer you allow assets to grow, the more they multiply beyond your imagination.

Consider this: if Jack had placed just $1,000 in safe investments at a modest 5% annual return in 1870, by today it would be worth more than **$60 million**. That is without alien artifacts, Torchwood's resources, or clever con artistry — just the patient discipline of allowing time to do the work.

This is why the Centuries Game matters. Wealth that outlives you is not the product of luck, but of building streams of income that flow long after you've stopped working.

Owning What Time Cannot Erase

Jack understands that some assets may rise and fall, but others endure across generations. He has always prioritized things that stand outside the trends of a single decade:

- **Land and Property**: Cities rise, borders change, but physical space remains valuable. A warehouse in 1900 becomes a skyscraper foundation in 2000.
- **Intellectual Property**: Ideas outlive their creators. Music royalties, books, films, YouTube content, and patents generate streams of income for decades. Jack would recognize that in today's world, a single viral song or a self-published book can outlast the person who made it.
- **Timeless Goods**: Art, rare collectibles, and precious metals maintain value no matter the century. The artifacts in Torchwood's Hub aren't just weapons — they're assets with infinite demand.

The key lesson: build ownership in things that do not vanish when the economy shifts. Let your wealth rest in assets that, like Jack himself, can adapt to the future.

The Quiet Investor's Path

Jack never flaunts all he owns. He could stride into any casino with a century's fortune in his back pocket, but that isn't his style. The Centuries Game is about **quiet ownership**, not loud consumption.

You don't need to look rich to be rich. In fact, appearing ordinary is one of the strongest shields for preserving and compounding wealth. Jack dresses well, lives stylishly, but never reveals the full depth of what he controls. That is the paradox: the less people know about your fortune, the more secure it becomes.

Intellectual Property: The Immortal's Modern Weapon

If Jack were navigating the 21st century as an ordinary human, his keenest eye would be on **intellectual property**. Unlike gold or land, intellectual property multiplies with every copy, stream, or download.

- **Music Royalties**: A single hit track recorded once can pay for lifetimes. Imagine compounding that with every technological shift — from vinyl to streaming.
- **YouTube Channels and Digital Content**: Once uploaded, videos generate income indefinitely. Even after the creator is gone, their work continues to produce.
- **Books and Publications**: Jack himself has the charisma to publish memoirs across eras, each generation rediscovering his "voice." For modern readers, self-publishing can create wealth that compounds invisibly.
- **Patents and Innovations**: Jack has seen thousands of inventions come and go. He would know the value of securing rights to an idea that others use for decades.

These assets mimic immortality: they allow ordinary people to build fortunes that continue paying out long after their own lifespans.

The Centuries Perspective

Jack's greatest gift isn't his immortality — it's his perspective. He knows the difference between money spent today and money compounded tomorrow. The secret is to stop asking, *"How much can I make this month?"* and start asking, *"What will this grow into fifty years from now?"*

This chapter invites you to play the Centuries Game:

- Invest as if you will live 150 years.
- Protect assets as if they must endure every war and collapse.
- Create intellectual properties as if the future will rediscover you.

Jack Harkness would tell you that your greatest ally is not luck, talent, or even genius. It is **time itself** — if you can learn to see wealth the way an immortal does.

Chapter 2: Glamour Without Exposure — The Art of Hidden Luxury

Captain Jack Harkness never needed to shout his wealth. Step into the Hub, and you see evidence of advanced technology, rare artifacts, and resources that could buy small nations. Yet, in his everyday presence, Jack walks the streets of Cardiff as just another man in a coat — a coat that has become his trademark. Stylish, yes. Expensive, perhaps. But never gaudy. Jack's true genius lies in balancing glamour with invisibility, living well without drawing the kind of attention that invites envy, theft, or unnecessary scrutiny.

The world worships visible wealth — sports cars, penthouses, extravagant vacations plastered across social media. But Jack plays a subtler game. He enjoys beauty, comfort, and luxury, but he conceals them beneath layers of charm, understatement, and quiet power. For him, **style is armor, not a billboard.**

The Signature Piece Principle

Jack's iconic military coat is more than just clothing. It is a lesson. He doesn't rotate through dozens of flashy outfits to prove affluence. Instead, he invests in one timeless, durable, recognizable piece that carries him through centuries.

This is the principle of the **signature piece**:

- One luxury item that defines your style without broadcasting wealth.
- A leather bag, a tailored suit, a unique watch, or a coat that becomes part of your identity.
- It sends the message of confidence and sophistication, without inviting questions like, *"How much did that cost?"*

The result: glamour that feels effortless, not performative.

The Art of Understated Luxury

Jack lives surrounded by alien artifacts, but you rarely see him flaunting them. He keeps most treasures hidden in Torchwood's vaults, using only what is necessary. The same principle applies to modern wealth: the richest people often live in comfortable, even luxurious environments — but without broadcasting their fortune to the world.

Practical applications:

- **Private Luxury, Public Simplicity**: Your home can be exquisite, but your public presence can remain humble.
- **Silent Symbols**: Choose quality items that only those "in the know" recognize. A hand-crafted fountain pen, a limited-edition book, or artwork known only to collectors.
- **Experiences Over Displays**: Travel to hidden paradises instead of competing in the Instagram race of crowded luxury resorts.

The quieter the luxury, the greater the enjoyment — and the longer it endures without envy tearing it down.

The Danger of Envy

Jack has lived long enough to see envy destroy empires. Wealth that is flaunted attracts enemies, while wealth kept discreet attracts security. Envy is one of the most corrosive forces in society — it invites jealousy, sabotage, even violence.

That's why Jack is careful:

- He builds trust through charm, not by showing off what he owns.
- He draws people to him with charisma and mystery, not wealth displays.
- He keeps enemies guessing.

The modern lesson? **Don't weaponize your wealth against others.** Keep it hidden, let it serve you, not your ego.

Building Quiet Influence

Jack never needed to flash cash to command respect. His authority comes from presence, charisma, and subtle positioning. Wealth, when hidden, can amplify these traits instead of overshadowing them.

How to build influence quietly:

- **Relationships First**: People remember how you made them feel, not what you wore or drove.
- **Resource Gatekeeping**: Like Jack controlling access to Torchwood's technology, hold quiet power by controlling resources others need.
- **Confidence Without Arrogance**: A calm, assured tone carries more weight than bragging about bank accounts.

True glamour is not in what you show, but in how you carry yourself.

The Immortal's Approach to Modern Luxury

If Jack were navigating the 21st century as a wealthy but secretive individual, he would adapt his strategy in ways that work for anyone today:

- **Digital Discretion**: Avoid oversharing online. Let your wealth flow behind the curtain of private accounts, trusts, or anonymous ownership.
- **Invisible Assets**: Real estate, intellectual property, private businesses — wealth that doesn't need to wear a label.
- **Savor Without Show**: A candlelit dinner in a hidden restaurant, a tailored coat, a first-class train journey — luxuries that feed the soul, not the crowd.

Jack's message is clear: if you want to live richly, live in a way that **satisfies you, not the world's applause.**

Conclusion: Glamour as a Cloak, Not a Spotlight

Jack Harkness is glamorous because he knows when to shine and when to fade into the background. His charm, his coat, his confidence — all are forms of wealth expressed without excess. The lesson for us is powerful: wealth is safest, and most satisfying, when it serves as a cloak, not a spotlight.

When you master the art of hidden luxury, you unlock freedom. Freedom from envy. Freedom from the need to prove yourself. Freedom to enjoy the richness of life without ever being trapped by the world's gaze. That is how Jack lives. That is how you can, too.

Chapter 3: Alien Artifacts and Modern Assets — Finding Hidden Value

Captain Jack Harkness has a talent for spotting treasure where others see trash. Inside the Torchwood Hub lie shelves of alien relics, fragments of technology, and artifacts dismissed as useless by those who don't understand them. Yet, in Jack's eyes, each holds potential — for defense, for leverage, for survival, or for unimaginable value in the right hands.

This ability to **see value where others overlook it** is one of Jack's most enduring secrets. Wealth doesn't always come from what everyone is chasing; it comes from recognizing the overlooked, the ignored, the "alien" in plain sight. You may not stumble across a time manipulator or a Chula warship, but you live in a world overflowing with hidden assets waiting to be discovered.

The Principle of the Overlooked

Every fortune begins with someone asking, *"What is everyone else ignoring?"* Jack mastered this principle by collecting alien artifacts, but the lesson applies to Earth's markets too. While the masses chase the obvious — trending stocks, luxury cars, flashy brands — the wise investor looks for:

- Assets undervalued today but destined for long-term growth.
- Items that seem ordinary but carry future scarcity.
- Technologies or ideas that are dismissed until the world catches up.

The overlooked often becomes the priceless.

Land: The Oldest Artifact of All

Jack has watched civilizations rise and fall around the same patches of earth. No matter how the world changes, land remains the ultimate hidden asset. Cities expand, industries grow, and suddenly the field no one wanted is the hub everyone needs.

Practical lessons:

- **Buy Where Growth Is Coming**: Study where infrastructure is planned — highways, airports, schools.
- **Hold Instead of Flip**: Wealth multiplies when you give land decades to appreciate.
- **Rural Gems**: Agricultural or remote land may seem valueless now, but in a resource-driven future, it becomes essential.

Jack's view: land isn't just dirt — it's history, power, and permanence.

Art and Collectibles: Cultural Relics with Hidden Power

Just as alien relics grow in value when context is understood, so too do human artifacts. Paintings, rare books, first-edition comics, and even trading cards become fortunes for those who buy before the world sees their worth.

- **Collect What Resonates**: True value often follows cultural significance.
- **Scarcity Matters**: Limited runs, discontinued items, or signed works compound value over time.
- **Digital Collectibles**: NFTs and blockchain-backed art mimic Jack's vault — ownership that transcends time and geography.

Jack knows one truth: today's oddity can be tomorrow's legacy.

Early-Stage Technologies: The Earthbound "Alien Tech"

When Jack examines alien gadgets, he isn't looking at what they are today — he imagines what they could become tomorrow. This mindset applies perfectly to early-stage technologies on Earth.

- **AI & Automation**: Tools that create content, streamline business, and design assets are today's alien relics. AI-generated books, music, or artwork can be turned into scalable income streams — products that keep selling long after you stop working.
- **Stocks in Emerging Fields**: Renewable energy, biotech, robotics, and space exploration often look speculative until they dominate entire industries. Buying early is like salvaging alien tech before the government notices.
- **Startups & Innovations**: Investing in small companies with disruptive potential mimics Jack's eye for hidden gadgets — risky at first, priceless if you choose well.

Creating Assets Out of Thin Air

Jack doesn't just collect — he *repurposes.* In the same way, modern wealth-builders can create valuable assets out of "nothing" using available tools:

- **Books & Media**: Self-publish books, guides, or stories. Digital platforms make it possible to earn royalties for decades from a single work.
- **YouTube & Content**: Videos uploaded today can keep generating income for years, much like a relic hidden in Torchwood's archives.
- **AI Creations**: Use AI to generate images, music, or educational tools, then package them as sellable products — intellectual property that keeps paying forward.
- **Online Courses & Patents**: Teaching skills or securing rights to inventions transforms personal knowledge into enduring revenue.

Just like alien tech, these assets don't wear out. They replicate, scale, and generate value across time.

Stocks: The Living Relics of Modern Capitalism

Stocks are like alien artifacts in motion — they're alive with risk, mystery, and explosive potential. Jack would approach them not with reckless gambling, but with his immortal patience:

- **Blue-Chip Foundations**: Companies built to last serve as "anchor artifacts."
- **Dividend Stocks**: Like relics that hum with energy, these pay out continuously.
- **Speculative Bets**: Just as Jack experiments with unknown tech, set aside a small portion for high-risk plays — biotech, AI, or spaceflight companies that could shape the future.

The secret isn't buying what's loud. It's buying what will matter **after decades of silence.**

The Torchwood Vault Mindset

In the Hub, Jack keeps artifacts in vaults, locked away, waiting for the right time. This is a model for modern wealth:

- **Accumulate**: Keep adding overlooked assets to your vault.
- **Secure**: Protect them with discretion, legal structures, and patience.
- **Wait**: The right moment always comes when others realize the value you saw first.

Wealth isn't just made in the buying. It's made in the waiting.

Conclusion: Seeing With Alien Eyes

Jack's greatest power isn't immortality — it's vision. He sees what others miss. He looks at broken tech and imagines a weapon. He looks at overlooked land and imagines a city. He looks at discarded relics and imagines a fortune.

For you, the lesson is simple: **train your eyes to see value in what others dismiss.**

The alien artifact of your life may be a digital product, a piece of land, a stock, or an idea. The world may laugh at it today, but in time, it may outlive you — and carry your wealth far into the future.

Chapter 4: Surviving Collapse — Outlasting Wars, Recessions, and Upheaval

Captain Jack Harkness has lived through the fall of empires, the collapse of currencies, and the destruction of entire worlds. He has seen banks turn to dust, kings stripped of crowns, and nations rewrite themselves overnight. To Jack, collapse isn't an "if" — it's a "when." And survival doesn't come from luck; it comes from preparation.

The truth is unsettling: no empire, economy, or system is permanent. The Roman Empire crumbled. The Great Depression shattered American wealth. Hyperinflation has destroyed currencies across history, from Weimar Germany to modern crises. Jack knows this better than anyone — and he knows how to **outlast the storm while others fall apart.**

The Principle of Resilient Wealth

Jack's survival tactic is simple: never put all your power in one fragile container. Just as he would never trust a single weapon or a single plan, you should never trust a single source of wealth. Resilient wealth means:

- **Diversity**: Spread assets across land, currency, intellectual property, and physical goods.
- **Mobility**: Have resources you can carry or access no matter where you are.
- **Patience**: When the world burns, fortunes are made by those who wait for the ashes to settle.

Resilient wealth doesn't chase trends; it prepares for collapse.

Diversifying Assets Like an Immortal

Jack knows that one empire's treasure becomes another's rubble. That's why he spreads value across categories:

- **Land & Real Estate**: Buildings may crumble, but the ground beneath remains.
- **Precious Metals & Tangibles**: Gold, silver, and commodities retain worth when paper money dies.
- **Cash Reserves**: In local collapses, liquid funds can buy time and opportunity.
- **Intellectual Property**: Royalties and copyrights continue to produce even when physical markets shrink.
- **AI & Digital Assets**: Content libraries, online businesses, and automated tools can outlast traditional disruptions.

Each layer is a shield. If one collapses, the others endure.

Hedging Against Volatility

Wars, pandemics, recessions — they all bring volatility. Jack doesn't gamble against it; he prepares for it.

Practical hedging strategies include:

- **Safe Havens**: Keep part of wealth in universally recognized stores of value (gold, stable foreign currencies).
- **Defensive Investments**: Utilities, food, water, and healthcare businesses often grow stronger in crises.
- **Alternative Incomes**: A book you wrote, a YouTube channel, or a patent doesn't depend on the local job market.
- **Flexible Assets**: Portable wealth — jewelry, art, cryptocurrency wallets — can move when borders close.

Jack would remind you: volatility is not the enemy. It's the signal that the rules are changing — and that fortunes are being transferred from the unprepared to the prepared.

Preparing for Systemic Resets

Jack has seen entire societies collapse, only to rebuild in new forms. For him, resets are inevitable. For you, preparation means staying positioned for the *next* world, not clinging to the *old*.

- **Stay Liquid**: Keep reserves to seize opportunities when prices crash.
- **Stay Flexible**: Train skills that adapt to any economy — writing, teaching, coding, repairing, trading.
- **Stay Informed**: Just as Jack gathers intelligence from alien species, you must track global trends, shifts in power, and signs of systemic strain.
- **Stay Invisible**: In upheaval, visible wealth invites theft or political seizure. Hidden wealth survives unnoticed.

Systemic resets punish the loud and reward the quiet.

The Survivor's Mindset

Jack's immortality isn't just physical. It's mental. He survives because he refuses to panic, refuses to cling, and refuses to assume that today's power will last tomorrow.

To adopt his mindset:

- **Detach from Normalcy**: Never assume "this will always be the way things are."
- **Expect Collapse**: Assume systems will fail — then structure your wealth to outlast them.
- **Turn Fear Into Opportunity**: Every collapse destroys wealth for many, but creates fortune for the few who are positioned correctly.

Jack sees collapse as a cycle, not an ending. And he always plays the long game.

Case Study: The Great Depression, Reimagined Through Jack's Eyes

If Jack were living through the 1930s, he would have:

- Held gold and silver when banks failed.
- Bought farmland when prices collapsed.
- Invested in companies with long-term potential (like Coca-Cola, IBM).
- Written books and media to keep earning royalties even during unemployment waves.
- Traveled lightly, able to move wealth discreetly across borders.

The lesson? The rules change in collapse, but the principles do not. Those who adapt thrive.

Conclusion: The Torchwood Blueprint for Endurance

Jack Harkness knows the truth most mortals ignore: **collapse is not the end, it is the reset button.** The only question is whether you're standing when the new world begins.

By diversifying assets, hedging against volatility, and preparing for systemic resets, you don't just survive upheaval — you position yourself to inherit the future.

Like Jack, you can walk out of the ashes not empty-handed, but carrying the seeds of the next empire. And that, more than anything else, is how wealth truly becomes immortal.

Chapter 5: Torchwood Tactics — Protecting What's Yours

Captain Jack Harkness knows better than most that having wealth or power is only half the battle. The other half is **keeping it safe.** Running the Torchwood Hub was not just about chasing aliens — it was about guarding secrets, safeguarding artifacts, and outsmarting enemies who would take what wasn't theirs. Jack's methods reveal a blueprint for protecting wealth in a world where danger often comes not from scarcity, but from exposure.

You may not be hiding a Weevil in Cardiff Bay or locking away alien technology in steel vaults, but the same principles apply to your finances. Wealth that isn't protected can vanish overnight — through theft, envy, legal disputes, inflation, bad partnerships, or government overreach. To win at the game of hidden fortune, you must master the art of defense just as fiercely as you pursue growth.

Secrecy: The First Layer of Defense

Jack thrives in shadows. He reveals what is necessary and withholds the rest. This is not paranoia — it is strategy. The less people know, the harder it is for them to target you.

Practical secrecy tactics:

- **Silent Accounts**: Keep separate reserves or trusts that don't sit in the spotlight of your main lifestyle.
- **Anonymous Ownership**: Where legal, use structures like LLCs, shell companies, or holding firms to keep your name out of property records.
- **Social Media Discipline**: Flaunting your wealth online is the fastest way to attract predators, creditors, or opportunists. Jack would never announce where his vault is. Neither should you.
- **Need-to-Know Principle**: Only disclose what is necessary, whether to friends, family, or even business partners.

Wealth that isn't seen cannot be targeted.

Structure: Building Fortresses Around Assets

The Torchwood Hub wasn't just a base — it was a fortress. Every door was sealed, every entry point layered with locks and codes. Jack's approach translates directly into how wealth should be structured.

- **Legal Fortresses**: Establish trusts, corporations, and estate plans that protect wealth from lawsuits, taxation shocks, or sudden emergencies.
- **Insurance Shields**: Property, business, and life insurance serve as barriers against unexpected loss.
- **Multi-Layered Storage**: Just as Torchwood didn't keep all alien artifacts in one room, you shouldn't keep all wealth in one bank, one account, or one form. Spread it. Protect it. Fortify it.
- **Redundancy Planning**: Have backups for everything — from digital files to safe deposits. If one vault falls, the others stand.

A fragile structure invites collapse. A layered structure ensures survival.

Strategic Alliances: The Power of Trusted Networks

Jack never operated alone. From Ianto to Gwen to Toshiko, Torchwood was built on alliances. These alliances weren't just friendships — they were **strategic partnerships** that amplified security and capability.

For protecting wealth, alliances matter:

- **Legal Allies**: A skilled lawyer can be the difference between losing everything and keeping it protected.
- **Financial Allies**: Accountants and advisors who understand discretion and long-term vision.
- **Practical Allies**: Trusted people who can step in if you are incapacitated — a spouse, sibling, or chosen partner with explicit roles.
- **Invisible Allies**: Quiet contacts in industries, communities, or governments who can warn you of threats before they arrive.

Wealth hidden in isolation is vulnerable. Wealth protected through trusted alliances is resilient.

Outsmarting Enemies: Thinking Like a Time Agent

Jack's past as a Time Agent taught him how predators think. He knows enemies rarely attack head-on; they exploit weakness, distraction, or arrogance.

How to outsmart your financial enemies:

- **Expect Betrayal**: Not everyone who smiles at you is a friend. Contracts, not promises, protect wealth.
- **Anticipate Pressure Points**: Governments raise taxes, competitors undercut, partners can sue. Prepare defenses before attacks come.
- **Stay Unpredictable**: Move assets, rotate strategies, avoid habits that make you an easy target.
- **Leverage Secrecy as a Weapon**: If others can't map your fortune, they can't attack it.

Enemies thrive on visibility. Jack thrives on mystery. You should too.

Modern Torchwood Tactics for Asset Protection

In today's world, you can apply Torchwood-style defenses in practical ways:

- **Digital Vaults**: Use encryption, offline backups, and secure servers for digital wealth.
- **Diversification Across Borders**: Consider accounts or holdings outside your home country for geopolitical protection.
- **Exit Strategies**: Always know how to liquidate or relocate assets quickly in case of sudden upheaval.
- **Phantom Income Streams**: Jack would love the concept of royalties, AI-generated content, or e-commerce — money that flows invisibly without revealing the true size of your wealth.

The more layers you add, the harder it becomes for collapse, theft, or envy to penetrate.

Conclusion: Guarding the Hub of Your Wealth

Jack Harkness knows that survival isn't just about having. It's about **holding**. Wealth is a fortress, and you are its guardian. If you fail to protect it, others will take it.

Torchwood tactics remind us that:

- Secrecy shields.
- Structure fortifies.
- Alliances defend.
- Strategy defeats enemies.

Your wealth doesn't need to be loud. It needs to be safe. By adopting Jack's methods — running your own life as though you were the keeper of an invisible Hub — you ensure that when others fall, you remain standing, surrounded by treasures no one can touch.

Appendix A: The 150-Year Investment Plan

A Sample Model for Building Intergenerational Wealth, Inspired by Jack's Long View

Captain Jack Harkness has survived revolutions, recessions, wars, and collapses because he thinks in centuries, not seasons. For him, wealth is not a quick grab — it is a **multi-generational fortress** that grows stronger with time. While you may not live for 150 years, you can build systems that allow your money, assets, and creations to outlive you, shaping prosperity for your children, their children, and even strangers who carry your legacy forward.

This appendix presents a **step-by-step model** for constructing an "immortal" wealth system — a framework designed to survive the unexpected, compound value quietly, and pass on resources in a way that grows across lifetimes.

Phase One (Years 1–20): Laying the Foundation

Think of this as the Torchwood recruitment stage — gathering the resources and tools that will protect you in crises.

- **Savings & Reserves**: Establish 6–12 months of living expenses in liquid accounts to survive recessions or job losses.
- **Income Diversification**: Build at least 2–3 income streams (a job, a side business, and a digital asset like a YouTube channel, self-published book, or online course).
- **Asset Acquisition**: Purchase your first real estate (even if modest) or acquire small amounts of gold, silver, or crypto as long-term hedges.
- **Intellectual Property Creation**: Begin producing content that generates royalties — books, patents, music, AI-generated tools. These are "modern alien artifacts" that continue paying forward.

Key Goal: Achieve stability and redundancy so no single crisis can wipe you out.

Phase Two (Years 20–50): Multiplying Assets

By now, Jack would be layering vaults with artifacts. You do the same with wealth.

- **Real Estate Expansion**: Acquire rental properties or agricultural land in growing regions. Land remains the most timeless store of value.
- **Business Ownership**: Launch or invest in businesses that produce cash flow beyond your direct labor.
- **Stocks & Funds**: Build a balanced portfolio with blue-chip companies, dividend-paying stocks, and index funds. Hold them long term to benefit from compounding.
- **Technology Bets**: Place small but consistent investments in emerging fields — AI, biotech, renewable energy, and space tech. One win can transform the future.
- **Cultural Collectibles**: Invest in rare art, books, comics, or cultural artifacts that can outlast fashion cycles.

Key Goal: Move from survival to compounding, building assets that appreciate and multiply without constant input.

Phase Three (Years 50–100): Fortifying the Vault

At this stage, Jack's Hub is filled with treasures, but always protected. Your wealth must now transition from growth to **resilience and protection**.

- **Trusts & Estate Structures**: Place assets in legal frameworks that outlast you, ensuring heirs or successors cannot squander them quickly.
- **Insurance Layers**: Protect real estate, businesses, and intellectual property from lawsuits or unforeseen disasters.
- **Phantom Incomes**: Focus heavily on royalties, licensing, and passive intellectual property streams. Ensure at least 50% of income flows from assets you no longer actively manage.
- **Global Diversification**: Store parts of wealth across borders, currencies, and systems. If one nation collapses, your legacy survives elsewhere.

Key Goal: Ensure that even if you vanish tomorrow, the system you built endures intact.

Phase Four (Years 100–150): Legacy & Immortality

Though you may not live to see this phase, your wealth can. This is where Jack's perspective — wealth that outlasts empires — becomes reality.

- **Intergenerational Transfers**: Pass on ownership of intellectual property, real estate, and businesses through structured trusts.
- **Education Funds**: Ensure heirs are trained to manage wealth wisely instead of wasting it. Build "Torchwood-style" training — mentoring them in secrecy, patience, and resilience.
- **Cultural Impact Assets**: Invest in works (books, inventions, art, AI tools) that continue to influence society long after you're gone.
- **Foundations & Philanthropy**: If desired, create organizations that extend your values into the future. Like Jack, leave a mark that transcends personal survival.

Key Goal: Transition your fortune from personal gain into a living system that thrives beyond your lifetime.

How to Create This System Today

You don't need to live 150 years to build a 150-year wealth engine. You need discipline, creativity, and patience. Begin with what Jack would call **alien-tech assets of the modern age**:

- **AI Tools**: Use AI to generate books, videos, or tools that create income with little ongoing effort.
- **Stocks & Land**: Buy and hold, thinking not in 5 years, but in 50.
- **Content Libraries**: Create digital vaults of intellectual property that can pay out forever.
- **Networks**: Build alliances with trusted partners, family, or successors who will guard what you've built.

Your wealth is not just money. It is a **Torchwood vault** of assets, artifacts, and structures that — if fortified correctly — can outlive you by centuries.

Final Thought

Captain Jack Harkness knows collapse will come, but he also knows the future belongs to those who prepare for it. The 150-Year Investment Plan is not about becoming a billionaire tomorrow. It is about playing the long game so that your fortune, like Jack himself, feels **immortal.**

Appendix B: The Immortal's Toolkit

Quick-Reference Guide to Stealth Wealth Practices

Captain Jack Harkness doesn't survive because he is loud about his power — he survives because he guards it in silence, deploys it with precision, and cultivates habits that outlast centuries. This toolkit distills his methods into actionable practices you can use to live richly while remaining invisible. Think of it as your **personal field kit for stealth wealth.**

1. Compounding Habits: The Immortal's Daily Discipline

Jack knows that survival is not built on one grand act, but on repeated small choices. Compounding applies not just to money, but to habits.

- **Save Consistently**: Even small daily savings, invested over decades, grow into empires.
- **Learn Relentlessly**: Read, study, and adapt. Knowledge compounds faster than money.
- **Health as Wealth**: Physical resilience ensures you can keep playing the game long after others burn out.
- **Invisible Investment**: Prioritize activities that quietly pay off — writing a book, recording a course, or acquiring land.

Quick Check: Did today's actions plant a seed for tomorrow's wealth?

2. Low-Profile Luxuries: Enjoying Without Exposure

Jack is stylish, charismatic, and magnetic — but he never reveals the true depth of his vault. Wealth is most satisfying when enjoyed privately.

- **Signature Item**: Choose one timeless piece (a coat, watch, pen) that defines your style without screaming wealth.
- **Private Comforts**: Invest in luxuries that feed your soul — a hidden retreat, fine bedding, quiet meals — not what feeds envy.
- **Experiential Wealth**: Focus on moments, not displays. A starlit walk, a hidden dinner, a first-class train ride feels richer than a Ferrari.
- **Silence as Status**: When others flaunt, stay quiet. Mystery builds more allure than exposure.

Quick Check: Would I enjoy this luxury just as much if no one ever saw it?

3. Diversification Checklist: The Torchwood Vault Model

Just as Torchwood never kept all alien relics in one vault, you should never rely on a single form of wealth. Diversification is defense.

- **Land & Property**: Secure ground that endures across centuries.
- **Stocks & Equities**: Anchor in blue-chips, branch into dividends, sprinkle speculative plays.
- **Precious Metals**: Gold, silver, or commodities for collapse scenarios.
- **Intellectual Property**: Books, patents, music, YouTube videos, AI-generated assets.
- **Digital Assets**: Crypto, domain names, online businesses.
- **Cash Reserves**: At least 6–12 months of liquidity.
- **Collectibles**: Art, rare editions, cultural artifacts with lasting scarcity.

Quick Check: If one vault were destroyed tomorrow, would the others survive?

4. Secrecy Strategies: Protecting the Invisible Fortune

Jack thrives in shadows. His enemies fail because they cannot map his resources. Wealth is safest when invisible.

- **Anonymous Structures**: Use trusts, LLCs, or holding companies for ownership.
- **Quiet Banking**: Spread accounts across institutions and, where legal, across countries.
- **Digital Shadows**: Encrypt files, use offline backups, and avoid oversharing financial wins online.
- **Need-to-Know Only**: Never tell anyone more than they must know. Even allies are safer with limited intel.
- **Phantom Income**: Build wealth streams that flow without your name attached — royalties, automated businesses, AI content libraries.

Quick Check: Could someone map my wealth from the outside? If yes, tighten security.

5. Emergency Protocols: The Collapse Survival Kit

Jack always has a plan when systems fail. You should too.

- **Portable Assets**: Jewelry, gold coins, hard drives, or encrypted wallets that can move with you.
- **Exit Strategies**: Know how to liquidate assets quickly if needed.
- **Alliances**: Build trusted networks of legal, financial, and practical allies.
- **Redundant Copies**: Keep duplicates of important documents and keys in separate secure locations.
- **Mental Resilience**: In collapse, the calm mind is the richest asset of all.

Quick Check: If my city shut down tomorrow, could I still access wealth within 48 hours?

Closing Note: Living Like Jack

The Immortal's Toolkit is not about becoming flashy, loud, or instantly rich. It is about building habits, assets, and shields that allow you to live with the confidence of Captain Jack Harkness: stylish but not reckless, wealthy but not obvious, immortal in preparation if not in flesh.

When you use these tools, you step into the same mindset Jack has carried since 1869: wealth that is safe, quiet, compounding, and waiting to serve you — no matter how the world changes.

Message from the Author:

I hope you enjoyed this book, I love astrology and knew there was not a book such as this out on the shelf. I love metaphysical items as well. Please check out my other books:

-Life of Government Benefits

-My life of Hell

-My life with Hydrocephalus

-Red Sky

-World Domination:Woman's rule

-World Domination:Woman's Rule 2: The War

-Life and Banishment of Apophis: book 1

-The Kidney Friendly Diet

-The Ultimate Hemp Cookbook

-Creating a Dispensary(legally)

-Cleanliness throughout life: the importance of showering from childhood to adulthood.

-Strong Roots: The Risks of Overcoddling children

-Hemp Horoscopes: Cosmic Insights and Earthly Healing

- Celestial Hemp Navigating the Zodiac: Through the Green Cosmos

-Astrological Hemp: Aligning The Stars with Earth's Ancient Herb

-The Astrological Guide to Hemp: Stars, Signs, and Sacred Leaves

-Green Growth: Innovative Marketing Strategies for your Hemp Products and Dispensary

-Cosmic Cannabis

-Astrological Munchies

-Henry The Hemp

-Zodiacal Roots: The Astrological Soul Of Hemp

- **Green Constellations: Intersection of Hemp and Zodiac**

-Hemp in The Houses: An astrological Adventure Through The Cannabis Galaxy

-Galactic Ganja Guide
Heavenly Hemp
Zodiac Leaves
Doctor Who Astrology
Cannastrology
Stellar Satvias and Cosmic Indicas
Celestial Cannabis: A Zodiac Journey
AstroHerbology: The Sky and The Soil: Volume 1
AstroHerbology:Celestial Cannabis:Volume 2
Cosmic Cannabis Cultivation
The Starry Guide to Herbal Harmony: Volume 1
The Starry Guide to Herbal Harmony: Cannabis Universe: Volume 2
Yugioh Astrology: Astrological Guide to Deck, Duels and more
Nightmare Mansion: Echoes of The Abyss
Nightmare Mansion 2: Legacy of Shadows
Nightmare Mansion 3: Shadows of the Forgotten
Nightmare Mansion 4: Echoes of the Damned
The Life and Banishment of Apophis: Book 2
Nightmare Mansion: Halls of Despair
Healing with Herb: Cannabis and Hydrocephalus
Planetary Pot: Aligning with Astrological Herbs: Volume 1
Fast Track to Freedom: 30 Days to Financial Independence Using AI, Assets, and Agile Hustles
Cosmic Hemp Pathways
How to Become Financially Free in 30 Days: 10,000 Paths to Prosperity
Zodiacal Herbage: Astrological Insights: Volume 1
Nightmare Mansion: Whispers in the Walls
The Daleks Invade Atlantis
Henry the hemp and Hydrocephalus

10X The Kidney Friendly Diet

Cannabis Universe: Adult coloring book

Hemp Astrology: The Healing Power of the Stars

Zodiacal Herbage: Astrological Insights: Cannabis Universe: Volume 2

Planetary Pot: Aligning with Astrological Herbs: Cannabis Universes: Volume 2

Doctor Who: Convergence Protocol – The Replicator War

Nightmare Mansion: Curse of the Blood Moon

The Celestial Stoner: A Guide to the Zodiac

Cosmic Pleasures: Sex Toy Astrology for Every Sign

Hydrocephalus Astrology: Navigating the Stars and Healing Waters

Lapis and the Mischievous Chocolate Bar

Celestial Positions: Sexual Astrology for Every Sign

Apophis's Shadow Work Journal: **:** A Journey of Self-Discovery and Healing

Kinky Cosmos: Sexual Kink Astrology for Every Sign

Digital Cosmos: The Astrological Digimon Compendium

Stellar Seeds: The Cosmic Guide to Growing with Astrology

Apophis's Daily Gratitude Journal

Cat Astrology: Feline Mysteries of the Cosmos

The Cosmic Kama Sutra: An Astrological Guide to Sexual Positions

Unleash Your Potential: A Guided Journal Powered by AI Insights

Whispers of the Enchanted Grove

Cosmic Pleasures: An Astrological Guide to Sexual Kinks

369, 12 Manifestation Journal

Whisper of the nocturne journal(blank journal for writing or drawing)

The Boogey Book

Locked In Reflection: A Chastity Journey Through Locktober

Generating Wealth Quickly:How to Generate $100,000 in 24 Hours

Star Magic: Harness the Power of the Universe

The Flatulence Chronicles: A Fart Journal for Self-Discovery

The Doctor and The Death Moth

Seize the Day: A Personal Seizure Tracking Journal

The Ultimate Boogeyman Safari: A Journey into the Boogie World and Beyond

Whispers of Samhain: 1,000 Spells of Love, Luck, and Lunar Magic: Samhain Spell Book

Apophis's guides:Witch's Spellbook Crafting Guide for Halloween

Frost & Flame: The Enchanted Yule Grimoire of 1000 Winter Spells

The Ultimate Boogey Goo Guide & Spooky Activities for Halloween Fun

Harmony of the Scales: A Libra's Spellcraft for Balance and Beauty

The Enchanted Advent: 36 Days of Christmas Wonders

Nightmare Mansion: The Labyrinth of Screams

Harvest of Enchantment: 1,000 Spells of Gratitude, Love, and Fortune for Thanksgiving

The Boogey Chronicles: A Journal of Nightly Encounters and Shadowy Secrets

The 12 Days of Financial Freedom: A Step-by-Step Christmas Countdown to Transform Your Finances

Sigil of the Eternal Spiral Blank Journal

A Christmas Feast: Timeless Recipes for Every Meal

Holiday Stress-Free Solutions: A Survival Guide to Thriving During the Festive Season

Yu-Gi-Oh! Holiday Gifting Mastery: The Ultimate Guide for Fans and Newcomers Alike

Holiday Harmony: A Hydrocephalus Survival Guide for the Festive Season

Celestial Craft: The Witch's Almanac for 2025 – A Cosmic Guide to Manifestations, Moons, and Mystical Events

Doctor Who: The Toymaker's Winter Wonderland

Tulsa King Unveiled: A Thrilling Guide to Stallone's Mafia Masterpiece

Pendulum Craft: A Complete Guide to Crafting and Using Personalized Divination Tools

Nightmare Mansion: Santa's Eternal Eve

Starlight Noel: A Cosmic Journey through Christmas Mysteries

The Dark Architect: Unlocking the Blueprint of Existence

Surviving the Embrace: The Ultimate Guide to Encounters with The Hugging Molly

The Enchanted Codex: Secrets of the Craft for Witches, Wiccans, and Pagans

Harvest of Gratitude: A Complete Thanksgiving Guide

Yuletide Essentials: A Complete Guide to an Authentic and Magical Christmas

Celestial Smokes: A Cosmic Guide to Cigars and Astrology

Living in Balance: A Comprehensive Survival Guide to Thriving with Diabetes Insipidus

Cosmic Symbiosis: The Venom Zodiac Chronicles

The Cursed Paw of Ambition

Cosmic Symbiosis: The Astrological Venom Journal

Celestial Wonders Unfold: A Stargazer's Guide to the Cosmos (2024-2029)

The Ultimate Black Friday Prepper's Guide: Mastering Shopping Strategies and Savings

Cosmic Sales: The Astrological Guide to Black Friday Shopping

Legends of the Corn Mother and Other Harvest Myths

Whispers of the Harvest: The Corn Mother's Journal

The Evergreen Spellbook

The Doctor Meets the Boogeyman

The White Witch of Rose Hall's SpellBook

The Gingerbread Golem's Shadow: A Study in Sweet Darkness

The Gingerbread Golem Codex: An Academic Exploration of Sweet Myths

The Gingerbread Golem Grimoire: Sweet Magicks and Spells for the Festive Witch

The Curse of the Gingerbread Golem

10-minute Christmas Crafts for kids

Christmas Crisis Solutions: The Ultimate Last-Minute Survival Guide

Gingerbread Golem Recipes: Holiday Treats with a Magical Twist

The Infinite Key: Unlocking Mystical Secrets of the Ages

Enchanted Yule: A Wiccan and Pagan Guide to a Magical and Memorable Season

Dinosaurs of Power: Unlocking Ancient Magick

Astro-Dinos: The Cosmic Guide to Prehistoric Wisdom

Gallifrey's Yule Logs: A Festive Doctor Who Cookbook

The Dino Grimoire: Secrets of Prehistoric Magick

The Gift They Never Knew They Needed

The Gingerbread Golem's Culinary Alchemy: Enchanting Recipes for a Sweetly Dark Feast

A Time Lord Christmas: Holiday Adventures with the Doctor

Krampusproofing Your Home: Defensive Strategies for Yule

Silent Frights: A Collection of Christmas Creepypastas to Chill Your Bones

Santa Raptor's Jolly Carnage: A Dino-Claus Christmas Tale

Prehistoric Palettes: A Dino Wicca Coloring Journey

The Christmas Wishkeeper Chronicles

The Starlight Sleigh: A Holiday Journey

Elf Secrets: The True Magic of the North Pole

Candy Cane Conjurations
Cooking with Kids: Recipes Under 20 Minutes
Doctor Who: The TARDIS Confiscation
The Anxiety First Aid Kit: Quick Tools to Calm Your Mind
Frosty Whispers: A Winter's Tale
The Infinite Key: Unlocking the Secrets to Prosperity, Resilience, and Purpose
The Grasping Void: Why You'll Regret This Purchase
Astrology for Busy Bees: Star Signs Simplified
The Instant Focus Formula: Cut Through the Noise
The Secret Language of Colors: Unlocking the Emotional Codes
Sacred Fossil Chronicles: Blank Journal
The Christmas Cottage Miracle
Feeding Frenzy: Graboid-Inspired Recipes
Manifest in Minutes: The Quick Law of Attraction Guide
The Symbiote Chronicles: Doctor Who's Venomous Journey
Think Tiny, Grow Big: The Minimalist Mindset
The Energy Key: Unlocking Limitless Motivation
New Year, New Magic: Manifesting Your Best Year Yet
Unstoppable You: Mastering Confidence in Minutes
Infinite Energy: The Secret to Never Feeling Drained
Lightning Focus: Mastering the Art of Productivity in a Distracted World
Saturnalia Manifestation Magick: A Guide to Unlocking Abundance During the Solstice
Graboids and Garland: The Ultimate Tremors-Themed Christmas Guide
12 Nights of Holiday Magic
The Power of Pause: 60-Second Mindfulness Practices
The Quick Reset: How to Reclaim Your Life After Burnout
The Shadow Eater: A Tale of Despair and Survival
The Micro-Mastery Method: Transform Your Skills in Just Minutes a Day

Reclaiming Time: How to Live More by Doing Less
Chronovore: The Eternal Nexus
The Mind Reset: Unlocking Your Inner Peace in a Chaotic World
Confidence Code: Building Unshakable Self-Belief
Baby the Vampire Terrier
Baby the Vampire Terrier's Christmas Adventure
Celestial Streams: The Content Creator's Astrology Manual
The Wealth Whisperer: Unlocking Abundance with Everyday Actions
The Energy Equation: Maximize Your Output Without Burning Out
The Happiness Algorithm: Science-Backed Steps to Joyful Living
Stress-Free Success: Achieving Goals Without Anxiety
Mindful Wealth: The New Blueprint for Financial Freedom
The Festive Flavors of New Year: A Culinary Celebration
The Master's Gambit: Keys of Eternal Power
Shadowed Secrets: Groundhog Day Mysteries
Beneath the Burrow: Lessons from the Groundhog
Spring's Whispers: The Groundhog's Prediction
The Limitless Mindset: Unlock Your Untapped Potential
The Focus Funnel: How to Cut Through Chaos and Get Results
Bold Moves: Building Courage to Live on Your Terms
The Daily Shift: Simple Practices for Lasting Transformation
The Quarter-Life Reset: Thriving in Your 20s and 30s
The Art of Shadowplay: Building Your Own Personal Myth
The Eternal Loop: Finding Purpose in Repetition
Burrowing Wisdom: Life Lessons from the Groundhog
Shadow Work: A Groundhog Day Perspective
Love in Bloom: 5-Minute Romantic Gestures
The Shadowspell Codex: Secrets of Forbidden Magick
The Burnout Cure: Finding Balance in a Busy World
The Groundhog Prophecy: Unlocking Seasonal Secrets
Nog Tales: The Spirited History of Eggnog

Six More Weeks: Embracing Seasonal Transitions
The Lumivian Chronicles: Fragments of the Fifth Dimension
Money on Your Mind: A Beginner's Guide to Wealth
The Focus Fix: Breaking Through Distraction
January's Spirit Keepers: Mystical Protectors of the Cold
Creativity Unchained: Unlocking Your Wildest Ideas in 2025
Manifestation Mastery: 365 Days to Rewrite Your Reality
The Groundhog's Mirror: Reflecting on Change
The Weeping Angels' Christmas Curse
Burrowed in Time: A Groundhog Day Journey
Heartbeats: Poems to Share with Your Valentine
Dino Wicca: The Sacred Grimoire of Prehistoric Magick
Courage of the Pride: Finding Your Inner Roar
The Lion's Leap: Bold Moves for Big Results
Healthy Hustle: Achieving Without Overworking
Practical Manifesting: Turning Dreams into Reality in 2025
Jurassic Pharaohs: Unlocking the Magick of Ancient Egypt and Dino Wicca
The Happiness Equation: Small Changes for Big Joy
The Confidence Compass: Finding Your Inner Strength
Whispers in the Hollow: Tales of the Forgotten Beasts
Echoes from the Hollow: The Return of Forgotten Beasts
The Hollow Ascendant: The Rise of the Forgotten Beasts
The Relationship Reset: Building Better Connections
Mastering the Morning: How to Win the Day Before 8 AM
The Shadow's Dance: Groundhog Day Symbolism
Cupid's Kitchen: Quick Valentine's Day Recipes
Valentine's Day on a Budget: Love Without Breaking the Bank
Astrocraft: Aligning the Stars in the World of Minecraft
Forecasting Life: Groundhog Day Reflections
Bleeding Hearts: Twisted Tales of Valentine's Terror
Herbal Smoke Revolution: The Ultimate Guide to Nature's Cigarette Alternative

Winter's Wrath: The Complete Survival Blueprint for Extreme Freezes.

The Groundhog's Shadow: A Tale of Seasons

Burrowed Insights: Wisdom from the Groundhog

Sensual Strings: The Art of Erotic Bondage

Whispered Flames: Unlocking the Power of Fire Play

Forgotten Shadows: A Guide to Cryptids Lost to Time

Six Weeks of Secrets: Groundhog Day's Hidden Messages

Shadows and Cycles: Groundhog Day Reflections

The Art of Love Letters: Crafting the Perfect Message

Romantic Getaways at Home: Turning Your Space into Paradise

Purrfect Brews: A Cat Lover's Guide to Coffee and Companionship

The Groundhog's Wisdom: Timeless Lessons for Modern Life

The Shadow Oracle: Groundhog Day as a Predictor

Emerging from the Burrow: A Journey of Renewal

The Language of Love: Learning Your Partner's Love Style

Authorpreneur: The Ultimate Blueprint for Writing, Publishing, and Thriving as an Author

Weathering the Seasons: Groundhog Day Perspectives

Valentine's Day Magic: A Guide to Romantic Rituals

The Shadow Chronicles: Stories of Groundhog Day

Love and Laughter: Fun Games for Valentine's Day

AstroRealty: Unlocking the Stars for Property Success

The Groundhog's Path: A Guide to Seasonal Balance

Groundhog Day Diaries: Reflections in the Shadow

The Groundhog's Light: Illuminating the Path Ahead

Valentine's Traditions from Around the World

AI Wealth Revolution: Unlocking the Trillionaire Mindset

Love Rekindled: Reigniting Passion in Relationships

Single and Thriving: Self-Love on Valentine's Day

Emerald Legends: Mystical Tales of Ireland

Green Alchemy: Harnessing Nature's Magic
The Hearts of Horror: A Valentine's Day Nightmare
The Leprechaun's Guide to Wealth and Wisdom
Dancing with the Sidhe: Celebrating the Otherworld
Shamrocks and Shadows: Mysteries of the Green Isle
Emerald Energy: Harnessing Luck and Growth
The Gingerbread Golem's Valentine: A Sweetheart's Guide to Love and Enchantment
The Celtic Knot: Weaving Life and Destiny
Green Fire: Elemental Magic for St. Patrick's Day
Clover Chronicles: Finding Your Inner Luck
Ireland's Mystical Creatures: A Field Guide
Gingerbread Golem's Love Almanac
Prowl and Thrive: The Lion's Guide to Success
Love Alchemy: Transforming Your Life Through Heart Energy
WORLD DOMINATION: Woman's Rule 3:The New Life
The Midnight Rose: A Guide to Lunar Love Spells
The Forbidden Letters: Writing Your Own Love Prophecy
Luck and Lore: St. Patrick's Day for Modern Mystics
The Green Path: A Pagan Celebration of Renewal
The Dark Architect's Guide to Reprogramming Reality
Prankster's Paradise: A Guide to Harmless Hijinks
Manifest Your Reality: The Law of Attraction Simplified
The TARDIS Owner's Manual: Understanding the Doctor's Ship: *A complete guide to the TARDIS, its technology, secrets, and mysteries*
Starlit Romance: Astrology Secrets for Finding True Love
The Time Lord's Atlas: A Complete Guide to the Whoniverse: ***A breakdown of the locations, planets, and dimensions explored in Doctor Who***
Sweetheart Shadows: The Dark Side of Love and Attraction
February Fire: Reigniting Passion in Every Area of Life

The Self-Love Toolkit: 5 Ways to Embrace Who You Are

February Sparks: Ignite Your Dreams in 28 Days

March to Success: A 31-Day Action Blueprint

Ancient Paths: The 13 Sacred Principles of Dino Wicca

Echoes of Tomorrow: Navigating the AI Revolution

The Wellness Blueprint: Balancing Mind, Body, and Soul

Green Horizons: Sustainable Living for a Better Tomorrow

The AI Wealth Code: How to Make Millions with Automation

AI-Powered Creativity: Writing, Art, and Music for Profit

Extinction Rites: Rebirthing Your Soul Through Prehistoric Magick

Sacred Serpents tarot

Celestial Enchantment blank journal

Star Strains

Culinary Journeys: Exploring Global Flavors at Home

The Hollowvale Curse

The Hollowvale Harvest

The Egg of Transformation: Awakening Your Inner Power

Blooming Into Power: A Wiccan Guide to Spring Awakening

The Nightmare Nexus: The Third Doctor's Perilous Haunting

Digital Detox: Reclaiming Your Life in a Connected World

Ostara's Path: Walking the Spiral of Renewal

The Sacred Hare

Financial Freedom: Building Wealth in the Modern Age

Spring's Cauldron: Stirring the Waters of Change

The Hollowvale Pact

Quantum Consciousness: The Science of Reality Shifting

The Hollowvale Hunger

The Sacred Waters Within: A Witch's Guide to Hydrocephalus Magick

The Raven's Nest: Building a Life of Unshakable Stability

AI and the Human Mind: The Future of Intelligence

The Hollowvale Reckoning

Timeless Love: Building and Maintaining Lasting Relationships

The Raven's Roar: Unlocking Unstoppable Confidence

Raven Sight: Awakening Intuition and Inner Wisdom

The Butterfly Effect: Small Changes, Big Transformations

Taming the Boogeyman: How to Conquer Your Inner Fears

The Magick of Green: Awakening Earth's Energy in You

The Entrepreneurial Mindset: Secrets to Business Success

The Hollowvale End

The Shadow Luck Ritual: Reclaiming Power from Your Dark Side

Spring Magick for Beginners: A Simple Guide to Seasonal Energy Work

Doctor Who: The Hollowvale Conundrum

The March of Miracles: Unlocking Synchronicities in Spring

Unveiling the Cosmos: A Guide to Stargazing and Space Exploration

The Ultimate Guide to Surviving an Economic Collapse

The AI Gold Rush: How to Profit from the AI Revolution

Bastet's Shadow: The Hidden Power of Feline Magick

The Bastet Codex: Unlocking the Goddess's Magickal Secrets

Purring Spells: Harnessing Bastet's Healing Frequencies

Bastet's Nine Lives: Rebirth, Transformation, and Immortality Spells

Primal Currents: Hydrocephalus Magick in the Path of Dino Wicca

The Digital Gold Rush: Mastering E-Commerce and Online Sales

Future Shock: Adapting to the Next Decade of Change

The Quantum Mindset: Think Like a Billionaire

Sacred Motherhood: Awakening the Divine Feminine Within

The Mother's Spellbook: Enchantments for Love, Protection, and Prosperity

The Witch's Guide to Parenting: Raising Empowered and Intuitive Children
The Magick of Motherhood: Reclaiming Your Power Through Rituals
The Pagan Path to Self-Love: A Goddess's Guide to Worth and Confidence
Wild Woman Magick: Unleashing Your Primal Power
The Money Magnet Blueprint: Unlocking Unlimited Wealth
Biohacking 101: Unlock Your Body's Full Potential
The Wild Father: A Pagan Guide to Strength and Wisdom
The Sacred Masculine: Unlocking Your Inner Power
The Druid's Compass
The Warrior's Mindset
The Father's Fire
Odin's Path
Ancestral Bonds
The House That Whispers
The Magician's Code
The Wild Hunt
The Green Man's Path
The Altar of Success
The Shadow and the Sword
The High Priestess's Guide to Energy Healing
The Lunar Mother
The Sacred Self-Care Grimoire
The Womb Wisdom Codex
The Wheel of the Mother
The Witch's Guide to Manifestation
The Q2 Reset
The Ultimate Guide to AI-Powered Passive Income
Escape the 9-5
AI Feline Fortunes
The Tear-Stained Grimoire

Razorblade Runes
Cemetery Sirens
The Midnight Wristwatch
The Town That Forgets
AI Horror & Creepypasta
The Hollow Frequency
The Breach Echo
The Quiet Between Worlds
The Sigil of Tharan-Khul
Summon the Vault of Y'ha'ten
The Becoming Codex
The Profit of Az'ra-nar
The Drowned Logos
Echoes of the Eldritch Will
The Deep Ledger
Necronomicon of Networth
Covenant of the Wealthwyrm
The Whisperer's Manifesto
The Rites of Azh-K'luth
The Ark of the Crawling Coin
The Tithe of Shadows
Inkheart Abyss
The Timewinds of Y'ha-nthlei
The Spiral Labyrinth of Azag-Nirrh
The Gallifreyan Heresy of the Black Pharaoh
The Psalms of Nyog-Sotha
Black Rain Alchemy
The Infinite Maw
The Entropic Blueprint
The Oracle of Sh'guul
The Book of Breach
The Drowned Saint's Testament
Dreamcraft of the Sleeper God

The Silence Market
Cthonomics: The Dark Wealth Algorithm
Invocation of the Ten-Eyed King
Wealthbound to the Wyrm Below
Become the Unnameable
Codex of the Sovereign Flame
Rituals of Relentless Becoming
The Shadow Ascends
The Eyes Beneath You
The Will That Wakes Worlds
Silence Is a Weapon
The Mirror That Screams
The Whisper Between Moments
The Mind That Devours Fear
The Myth of the Finished Self
The Architect of Your Madness
The Voice You've Buried
The Discipline of Madness
Stormborn: Awakening Your Inner Tempest
The Mind That Ate Time
Unbind Your Becoming
The Pact You Owe Yourself
The Devourer's Diet
The Acid That Carves the Path
The Tower You Must Burn
The Breath Between Worlds
Speak Like the Deep
The Labyrinth Within
The Spine of the Sea God
Rejection Is a Portal
The Crown You Refused
The Scar Is the Spell
The Lightless Flame

The Habit of Becoming Horrific
ChickenJockey Chaos
The Gatekeeper Within
You Are Not Your Name
The Compass of the Mad
The Archive of Unsent Letters
What the Mirror Can't Show You
The Knife You Needed
Worship Nothing, Become Everything
The Other Voice
The Body the World Forgot
The Vein of the Void
The Black Bone Codex
The Puzzle of the Hidden Self (Millennium Puzzle)
The Eye That Sees the Lie *(Millennium Eye)*
The Ring of Return (Millennium Ring)
The Rod of Relentless Will ***(Millennium Rod)***
The Tally of the Soul (Millennium Tauk/Necklace)
The Key to the Locked Timeline (Millennium Key)
The Scale of Sacred Decisions (Millennium Scales)
Inferno Bites: The UnOfficial Minecraft Lava Cookbook
Rot in the Attic
Prana: The Hidden Force of Your Infinite Self
The Shadow Realm Within: Transforming Darkness Into Destiny
The Borderland Collapse
Claws of Protection: Bastet's Defensive Magick
Mr. Ring-a-Ding's Madness
Yugioh Astrology: Celestial Deckcraft and Duel Destiny (2026–2027 Edition)
The Seal You Signed: Unlocking the Power You Once Feared
The Puzzle of Infinite Minds: Unlocking the Mentalism Hidden Within

The Eye That Mirrors the All: Secrets of Inner Reflection

Doctor Who: The Toymaker's Broadcast

The Rod of Eternal Flow: Commanding the Currents of Vibration

Golden Eyes of Bastet: Enhancing Psychic Vision

The Key of Dual Forces: Balance Within the Polarity

The Scales of Living Rhythm: Timing the Dance of Life

The Necklace of Hidden Cause: Weaving the Webs of Fate

The Ring of Secret Masters: Rising Through the All Within All

Daggers of the Dying Deep

Bastet's Wealth and Fortune Magick: Prosperity Rituals of the Goddess

The Tide that Speaks

The Scrolls of Petosiris: 13 Rituals from the Feathered Eye

Petosiris and the Living Plague of Osirion

Feline Fire: Bastet's Passion and Love Magick

The Star Altar of Petosiris

Bastet's Whiskers: Supernatural Sensory Magick

The Bastet Grimoire

Feeding the Shadows

The Mouthless Prayer

The Spiral Wound

Becoming the Ibis: Lessons from Petosiris's Mind

The Crimson Coven: Cola Magick for Sweet Dominion

Sacred Cat's Paw

The Soda Zodiac: A Flavor for Every Sign

Covenant of the Crawling Flame

The Ink of Ish'Zur

Frothroot: The Thirst That Ate the World

The Golden Glyphs of Prosperity

The Etherbind Codex

Echoes of the Resistance: Reclaiming the You That Survived

Harnessed Minds: Breaking Free from Mental Control
The Eyes in the Smoke
Rootwake: The Carbon Covenant
Skitter Logic: Unlearning the Fear That Built You
Doctor Who: The World That Froths
Rootwake: The Fizz That Rewrites Flesh
Rootwake: Frothfather of the World
The Holly Pact: Blood Beneath the Mistletoe
The 2nd Mass Principle: Building Unbreakable Tribes
Web of Wits: A Survival Guide to Encounters with Anasi the Spider (Aunt Nancy)
The Hexbreaking Handbook: Effective Spells to Remove Curses
Pop Alchemy: Transform Your Life One Sip at a Time
The Mason Code: Leading in Unleadable Times
Petosiris and the Fifth Chamber of Thoth
The Ether Seed Within
The Parent of Tomorrow
Petosiris's Pyramid of Perpetual Wealth
Unlearn the World
Grimoire of the Hollow Tongue
Zodiac Weeds: Finding Your Strain Through the Stars
Aquarius Rises in the Bank
The Sugar God's Smile
The Skinclock Reversal: Biohacking the Face of Time
Debtburn: How to Obliterate What You Owe Forever
The Ice Cream Oracle: What Your Cone Says About Your Future
Silence Is Sovereignty: The Power of Being Unreadable
The Wind That Whispers Through Stone
Path of the Four Directions
Doctor Who: The Maestro's Symphony of Endings
Oxygen Grail: Breathing to Undo the Clock

Zodiacal Collapse: When Stars Devour Time
Teachings from the Red Sand Silence
Doctor Who: Omega – The Broken Equation
Memory Wipe Your Past: Start Over Like a MiB
Mitochondria Prime: Ignite the Core of Youth
A Nest of Roaches
Grub from the Galaxy: MiB Recipes You'll Never Forget
Whiskers of Power: Bastet's Guide to Inner Sovereignty
The Gift Must Cost Them: Negotiation Through Unequal Exchange
The Worm Guys' Wealth Code: Hustle Like an Alien
Bug Out: The Edgar Method for Ruthless Goal Setting
Weaving Life with Spiderwoman's Pattern
Doctor Who: The Rani's Renaissance
How to Get a Job (If You're a Puppygirl)
Speak Through Others: The Art of Proxy Power
T-Rex Your Trauma: Reclaim the Power of Your Primal Self
The Black Briefcase: How MiB Stay Wealthy in Silence
The Thirst Beyond Reason: Understanding Diabetes Insipidus From the Inside Out
Backwoods Witchcraft for Billionaires: The Pagan Path from Dirt Roads to Gold Roads
The Moonshine Grimoire: Fermented Spells for Abundance
The Nameless Geometry
The Wraith's Mixtape: Spellcasting with Songs of Sorrow
The Gallifreyan Gentleman: Silent Wealth, Sonic Confidence, and the Doctor's Code of Living
Sugar Water Confidence
Dino Totems: Spirit Guides from Earth's First Gods
Pumpkin Sigils & Ritual Smoke
The Hózhó Compass
The Distortus Discipline – Order from Inner Mutation
Witchcraft for the Cold-Blooded Soul

Moonlight Over the Blessingway
Water, Interrupted: When the Body Forgets How to Hold On
Deformed but Divine: Embracing Your Asymmetry
Hexes in the Henhouse: The Farm Witch's Guide to Power
The Reversed Flame: A Grimoire of Inverted Power
Salt, Cells, and Sanity: Reclaiming Balance with Diabetes Insipidus
King of the Broken: Crowning the Flawed Self
Moonlight Scars: Emo Moon Magick and the Art of Lunar Sorrow
Noose Spells: Magick of the Hanging Rope
The Goth Cathedral: Rituals of the Broken and Beautiful
The Cretaceous Codex: Dino Spirits and Fossil Magick
The Turkey Bones Ritual
Nine Lives of Manifestation: Unlocking Bastet's Reality Codes
Chaos Muscles: Building Strength from Twisted Pain
Emo Blood Magick: The Veins of Power
The 3AM Flood: Nighttime Urination, Sleep Loss, and the DI Spiral
The Silence Between the Stars
The Lemon Method: Sour Your Way to Success
Starlit Sovereign
The Rite of Twelve Gates: Walking the Gates of the Duat.
Cornbread and Conjure: Recipes for Riches and Rootwork
The Black Rose Rituals: Emo Love Spells and Obsession Magick
The Eternal Goodbye: Death Magick and Rebirth Rituals
Sinkrot: The Drain That Remembers
The Hybrid Mindset: Thinking Beyond Evolution
Bone Dry: Navigating Dehydration Before It Breaks You
Wreathcraft: Winter Sigils and Yuletide Spells
The Rite of Twelve Mouths

S'mores of the Damned: Haunted Recipes for Halloween Night

Rethink the Drink: A Beverage Survival Guide for DI Warriors

The Shadow Chord: Guitar Magick and Sonic

Malformed Yet Majestic: Leading When You Feel Wrong Inside

The Cursed Diary: Ink-Stained Spells of the Emo Soul

Anxiety Off Switch: Emergency Reset for a Fried Nervous System

The Energy Heist: How to Take Back Your Life from Drainers

Beyond the Bathroom: Rebuilding Your Social Life With DI

Coyote's Gift for Decision Makers

Ghoul-Goo: Spooky S'mores You'll Die For

Echoes in the Mirror: Scrying and Self-Destruction Magick

Thread and Thorn: Stitching Spells from Rural Cloth

The Mogwai Mind: Building Untouchable Wealth from Small Ideas

Be Your Own Guide: Trust Your Inner Compass

Hormones in Chaos: The Endocrine Puzzle of Diabetes Insipidus

ChronoCleanse: Detox Your Biological Timeline

The Limb You Hide Is the One That Saves You

Leaves, Bones, and Whisper Spells

The Dinosaur Mindset: Prehistoric Tactics for Modern Wealth

Clawing Back Control: A Bastet Method for Boundaries and Empowerment

Samhain Codes of the Forgotten

Orange Alchemy: The Autumnal Spellbook

Monster Within, Master Without

The Sigil That Sleeps

Hearthcraft: Yule Hearth Sigils and Winter Warmth Spells

Temple of the Purring Moon: Rituals from Bastet's Lineage
When the Earth Remembers Your Footsteps
Food for Mood: Eat to Heal Depression, Not Just Survive It
Witch of the Kudzu Vine: Southern Pagan Wealth Secrets
The Invisible Diagnosis: Advocating for Yourself With DI
The Coffin's Lullaby: Sleep Magick and Nightmares as Portals
Ashes of the Will: Rituals for Erasing the Self
The Fracture Rite: Shattering the Magickal Core
Funeral Candles: The Art of Emo Flame Magick
The Black Grimoire: A Blank Ritual for Writing in Absence
Phantom Thirst: A Halloween Survival Guide for Diabetes Insipidus
The Hollow Crown: Emo Royalty and Magick of the Outcast King
Sandpainting for the Soul
Falling Into Balance: Using the Extra Hour to Recalibrate Life
100 Southern Superstitions That Still Work
The DI Child: A Parent's Guide to Raising Hydrated, Happy Kids
The Jungle of Shame: Escaping the Hidden Lab of Doubt
The Witch's Toast: S'mores Spells and Creepy Confections
The Hoodoo Pantry: Spells from the Mason Jar

Get Some Tarot cards: https://www.makeplayingcards.com/sell/apophis-occult-shop

Get some shirts: https://www.bonfire.com/store/apophis-shirt-emporium/

Instagrams:
@apophis_enterprises,
@apophisbookemporium,
@apophisscardshop
Twitter: @apophisenterpr1
Tiktok:@apophisenterprise
Youtube: @sg1fan23477
Hive: @sg1fan23477
CheeLee: @SG1fan23477

Podcast: Apophis Chat Zone: https://open.spotify.com/show/5zXbrCLEV2xzCp8ybrfHsk?si=fb4d4fdbdce44dec

Newsletter: https://apophiss-newsletter-27c897.beehiiv.com/

If you want to support me or see posts of other projects that I have come over to: **buymeacoffee.com/mpetchinskg**

I post there daily several times a day

Get your Dinowicca or Christmas themed digital products, especially Santa Raptor songs and other musics. Here: **https://sg1fan23477.gumroad.com**

Apophis Yuletide Digital has not only digital Christmas items, but it will have all things with Dinowicca as well as other Digital products.

www.ingramcontent.com/pod-product-compliance
Lightning Source LLC
LaVergne TN
LVHW022024200926
848481LV00007B/2524
9798349547362